The My[...] [...]e Wizard Clip

By Raphael Brown

Loreto Publications
Fitzwilliam, NH 03447
AD 2010

Published by
Loreto Publications
P. O. Box 603
Fitzwilliam, NH 03447
Phone: 603 239 6671
www.LoretoPubs.org

Table of Contents

Foreword:

Concerning Extraordinary Mystical Phenomena

1. Extraordinary Divine Phenomena

2. Diabolical Phenomena

With regard to the first type, Extraordinary Divine Phenomena; it is divided into those of the intellectual order, and those of the psycho-physiological order.

a.) Divine intellectual phenomena may be either private revelations or charismas. The first type are chiefly for the benefit of the recipient, the latter are chiefly for the benefit of others.

Examples of private revelations are those received by Saint Joseph, Saint Paul and those received by Saint Theresa of Avila. To know true revelations, it is necessary to know the object, the effects, and the signs which accompany them. The church accepts no revelations except after long and careful investigation, and even then she does not force them on the faithful. With regard to charismas Saint Paul in the first Epistle to the Corinthians, Chapter XII, distinguishes nine.

b.) Psycho-physiological phenomena — such as affect both the soul and body, and which are more or less related to ecstasy. The principal of these are levitation, luminous rays, fragrant odors, prolonged fasting, and stigmatization. The difference between these and psycho-neurotic phenomena are found in (a) the persons themselves, (b) in the diversity of the phenomena (peace and rapture of the soul intimately united with God rather than convulsions, spasms, etc.) in the results, steady mental growth, increase in love of God, devoted service to neighbors. With regard to the second type of Extraordinary Phenomena, i.e., Diabolical Phenomena, we may divide them into two classes: 1. Obsession, 2. Possession.

With regard to obsession: This consists in a series of unusually violent and persistent temptations. It is called external when the temptations affect the exterior senses by means of apparitions, and internal when they stir up sensations or emotions. There are examples of obsessions among the saints, e.g., Saint Alphonsus Rodriguez, Saint Catherine of Sienna, Saint Francis Xavier, Saint Theresa of Avila, the Curé of Ars.

As to Possession: Two elements constitute possession; the presence of the devil in the body of the possessed, and the dominion exercised by the devil over that body, and through it over the soul. There are three principal signs by which possession may be recognized: Speaking an unknown tongue or understanding it when spoken by another; making known distant and hidden things; exhibiting a strength out of all proportion with one's age and circumstances.

The special remedy is found in the exorcisms (formulas of prayer prepared by the church for priests delegated by their bishop in cases where the fact of possession has been ascertained).

Note: The foregoing is a synopsis of book III chapter III, *The Spiritual Life* by Adolph Tanquerey, S.S., Desclee & Co., Tournai (Belgium) 1932, pp. 700-726.

In *A Companion to The Summa*, Sheed and Ward, 1941, Vol. I, Page 425, Father Walter Farrell, O. P., comments:

"Now and then, buy rarely, the devil makes a spectacular display by attacking men physically. This might be of great importance for advertising purposes, if the devil needed advertising; it has little importance from any other point of view. Three classes of these physical attacks have been distinguished by theologians, ascending to a climax of impotent fury. The first, called infestation, consists of an attack centering on the surroundings of man rather than himself; noise-making, throwing things about, breaking articles of furniture, mysterious knocks on doors and walls, and so on. It was this sort of thing that plagued the Curé of Ars night after night during the pitifully few hours he could set aside for sleep. Obsession, on the contrary, is a personal attack, but essentially an exterior attack directed to physical injury and so to be instilling of terror; in its effects, it does not go beyond the attack that any man might make on another by blows or kicks."

The phenomena of infestation, as described above, are usually known in modern psychical research as "poltergeists," from a German term meaning racket-making spirits. According to the *Encyclopedia Britannica,* "cases of this kind have been recorded for many hundreds of years, and from all parts of the world." Sixteen centuries ago Saint Augustine narrated in his great work *The City of God* (Book 22 Chapter 8) the following case of infestation which strikingly resembles the first part of the story of the Wizard Clip:

"Hesperius, a neighbor of ours, has a farm, and finding that his family, his cattle, and his servants were suffering from the malice of evil spirits, he asked our priests, during my absence, that one of them would go with him and banish the spirits by his prayers. One went, offered there the Sacrifice of the Body of Christ, praying with all his might that the vexation might cease. It did cease immediately, through the mercy of God."

Thus, pending a formal judgment of church authorities concerning the mysterious events known as the Wizard Clip, it would appear that the destructive phenomena may have been another example of infestation by poltergeists, which were in due time completely banished and exorcised by the celebration of a Holy Mass and by the prayers of a Catholic priest in the infested house.

The subsequent instructions and revelations by the invisible voice, on the other hand, may constitute yet another instance of divine extraordinary phenomena of the intellectual order, as outlined above, essentially similar in origin, nature and effects, to the mystical communications which are known to have occurred in the lives of countless saintly men and women during every century in the history of the Catholic Church. It is certainly of primary significance that the final result in this case was the conversion of a number of persons to the true faith.

Conclusion: Extraordinary Mystical Phenomena are by no means essential to the spiritual life, nor are they to be desired or sought after. Saint Paul in I Corinthians, Chapter XIII, says:

> If I should speak with the tongues of men and of angels, but do not have charity, I have become as sounding brass or a tinkling cymbal. And if I have prophecy and know all mysteries and all knowledge, and if I have all faith so as to remove mountains, yet do not have charity, I am nothing. And if I distribute all my goods to feed the poor, and if I deliver my body to be burned, yet do not have charity, it profits me nothing.
>
> Charity is patient, is kind; charity doe not envy, is not pretentious, is not puffed up, (is not ambitious, is not self seeking, is not provoked; thinks no evil,) does not rejoice over wickedness, but rejoices with the truth; bears with all things, believes all things, hopes all things, endures all things.

Catholic Historical Society
Diocese of Richmond

Acknowledgments

The author wishes to express his grateful acknowledgment for assistance in the preparation of this booklet to the Right Reverend Edward P. McAdams, the Reverend William C. Repetti, S. J., the Reverend William T. Winston, the Reverend John Tracy Ellis, the Reverend Paul Cadden, O.S. B., the Reverend Valentine J. Koehler, O. S. B., the Reverend Paul L. Love, the Reverend Thomas C. Healey, Mr. and Mrs. John J. Daly, Miss Helen C. Schaarman, and last but not least Miss Emma B. Lynch.

In conformity with the decrees of Pope Urban VIII, the author formally declares that the preternatural or seemingly supernatural facts recorded in this historical narrative rest on purely human authority, and consequently he does not in any way intend to pronounce a final judgment, or to anticipate any future decision of lawful Church authority as to their nature.

The Mystery of the Wizard Clip

At Middleway, West Virginia

"One of the most wonderful manifestations of God's benevolence during the struggles of the primitive Church in these United States . . ." such is the impressive estimate of the learned Jesuit scholar, Father Joseph M. Finotti, concerning the extraordinary but little known spiritual drama which took place one hundred and fifty years ago near Martinsburg, West Virginia. And the Reverend Charles I. White, formerly pastor of Saint Matthew's in Washington, referring to this incident in his essay on the history of the Catholic Church in America, made the following significant comment: ". . .supernatural events had. . . been permitted by the Almighty. . . which are worthy of record, inasmuch as they tend to confirm and illustrate the famous saying of Saint Thomas Aquinas, that God would send an angel, if necessary, to instruct in the faith those who sincerely seek after it by making a right use of the gifts of nature."

And in fact, in the year 1797, on a farm near the present Middleway, Jefferson County, West Virginia, a Lutheran family was saved from diabolical persecutions by a Catholic priest and then instructed in the Catholic religion by a mysterious, invisible voice from the other world, that continued for seventeen years to enlighten, guide and inspire these former protestants and their Catholic friends to live as fervent and model Christians. Frequently during those years, this mystic voice, whose "influence was always beneficial," communicated timely warnings, prophecies, and messages of charity and mercy for many persons, which resulted in numerous conversions.

The Mystery of the Wizard Clip

That such seemingly miraculous phenomena did actually take place has never been questioned by serious historians, and furthermore their existence was irrefutably confirmed at the time not only by several local priests but also by two of the foremost figures in the Catholic Church in America in those years: Archbishop John Carroll of Baltimore and the Reverend Prince Gallitzin. In addition, the great Catholic historian John Gilmary Shea devoted to the subject over two pages in his monumental *History of the Catholic Church within the United States* (New York, 1888), in which he declared that "strange and wonderful as the main facts related are, they were credited after careful examination by able, learned, and far from credulous men." And according to the scholarly Professor P. J. Mahon, in his *Trials and Triumphs of the Catholic Church in America* (Chicago, 1907), "no facts are better substantiated." Non-Catholic authorities also confirm the truth of events. In 1904 an article in *The West Virginia Historical Magazine* admitted that "the people there had no doubt of the facts related." And as recently as 1941 the West Virginia guidebook of the American Guide Series compiled by the Writers' Program of the Works Project Administration gave nearly a whole page to an objective account of the locally famous Mystery of the Wizard Clip.

We shall not narrate the principal incidents of this fascinating and significant chapter in the early history of the Catholic Church in the United States, for the most part in the same words as they are recorded by eye witnesses and by the children of eye witnesses in Father J. M. Finotti's valuable collection of documents entitled *The Mystery of the Wizard Clip* (Baltimore, 1879, p. 143).

Holy Scripture teaches us "it is honorable to reveal and confess the works of God" (Tob. 12:7). And it is our hope and prayer that many American Catholics — and non-Catholics too — may come to share

The Mystery of the Wizard Clip

Father Finotti's conviction that this stirring historical narrative "draws our heart near to God, it teaches lessons of supernatural wisdom. . .The Finger of God is here! . . . Herein lies the beauty of the story."

The historical existence of the principal character in our drama is definitely established by the first official Census of Heads of Families in the State of Pennsylvania in 1790 (Washington, 1908, p.287), according to which there resided in York County in that year a man named Adam Livingston, who was the head of a household of twelve other persons, including four slaves.

The McSherry family tradition states that Adam Livingston was an honest and industrious Lutheran who owned considerable property in York County, Pennsylvania. Due to mysterious causes, however, his property began to diminish in various ways: his barn burned down, and his horses and cattle died.

As these losses continued, Livingston and his family decided to move. Early in the 1790's, therefore with his second wife and several children, he left Pennsylvania and migrated to the lower end of the lovely Shenandoah Valley, where he settled on a large estate of the triangle formed by Charles Town, Martinsburg, and Winchester, all of which were then in the state of Virginia.

But there too the same mysterious forces continued to afflict the Livingston household. There too the cattle and horses died. Now the very house in which Adam and his wife and children lived seemed to have become haunted: at night they were kept awake by weird noises, such as loud knocks and rumblings as of galloping horses and wagons. But even in daylight their furniture would be suddenly banged about and their crockery smashed onto the floor by invisible hands. Chunks of fire rolled out of the beds across the rooms. At times the heads and legs of chickens and geese were seen to drop off suddenly. But by far the most sensational of these devilish afflictions was the stranger persistent clipping and cutting that attacked almost every piece of cloth and leather on the Livingston estate. Sheets, tablecloths, shirts, dresses, suits, and even leather boots and saddles, whether in use or locked up in closets, were skillfully slit and clipped into crescent shaped strips by invisible shears! The noise of the scissors clipping merrily away was distinctly heard on many occasions by different members of the family.

Soon the whole countryside was talking about the mysterious "Wizzard Clip" at the Livingston's place, which eventually came to be known as "Cliptown" — a name which is still in use locally. One old lady in Martinsburg, wishing to satisfy her curiosity, went to visit the Livingstons, but before entering the haunted house she carefully took off her new silk hat and wrapped it in her large handkerchief, to save it from being clipped. Upon leaving, however, she found her new hat was cut into small ribbons!

Poor old Mr. Livingston's mental torture was acute, and he turned to the Bible for help against these attacks which were clearly diabolical. As Father Gallitzin later wrote, "The good old man reading in his Bible that Christ had given to His ministers power over evil spirits, started from his home to Winchester in Virginia, and having, with tears in his eyes, related to his minister the history of his distress, losses, and sufferings, begged of him to come to his house and exercise in his favor the power he had received from Jesus Christ. The parson candidly confessed that he had no such power. The good old man. . . therefore rationally concluded that Parson S- could not be a minister of Christ. . . and applied to other persons calling themselves ministers of Christ, some of whom promised relief. They came, prayed, and read; but they prayed and read in vain . . ."

As a result of so many disappointments, Mr. Livingston almost came to the conclusion that Christ no longer had any true ministers on earth. So in desperation he turned to some local conjurers or magicians, one of whom promised to banish the evil spirit if paid a good sum in advance, but refused the job when the shrewd old farmer offered to pay him double that amount — after he succeeded! Three others came very confidently from Winchester, but took to their heels when they saw a large stone whirl around the living room without any support for fifteen minutes!

According to Father Gallitzin, just when Adam Livingston "was determined, henceforward, never to apply to any one of them calling themselves ministers of Christ," it happened that "a Roman Catholic peddler" who spent the night in the Livingston home and who "was much disturbed by the noise, which prevailed almost the whole night in the house, tried to persuade Livingston to send for a Roman Catholic priest, but Livingston answered quickly that he had tried so many of those fellows, he was not going to try and more of them."[1]

[1] According to a local tradition, the peddler is alleged to have died in Livingston's home, after the Lutheran farmer had refused to send for a priest to administer the last sacraments to the Catholic peddler and then, apparently as a direct result, the haunting is said to have commenced. This tradition, however, would seem to be unreliable, for the following reasons: 1. Mrs. Anastasia McSherry declared that the mysterious phenomena had begun in Pennsylvania; 2. Father Gallitzin's letter of April 11, 1839, as quoted above, demonstrated clearly that the phenomena had begun before the peddler's visit; and 3. Neither Father Gallitzin nor any of the eyewitnesses mentioned the peddler's death. It is quite understandable that in the early years, before a correct account of the events was available in print, an oral tradition may have confused the peddler's urging Livingston to send for a priest, in order to exorcise the house, with the more usual reason for calling in a priest, namely upon the approach of death. John T. Reily, the distinguished Catholic regional historian, wrote in his detailed analysis of the Wizard Clip story that there is no evidence that the peddler fell sick and died in the Livingston home. Modern scholars whom the writer has consulted agree that that version of the event is not substantiated.

And then one night Mr. Livingston had a strange dream. He dreamed that he was climbing up a high mountain, struggling up with great difficulty, clinging to roots and bushes. When he finally reached the top, he saw a beautiful church and in it a "minister dressed in peculiar robes" and he heard a voice say to him "that is the man who can relieve you!" His wife, hearing him groan in his sleep, woke him up, and after talking over the dream, he decided to search that same morning for the minister dressed in robes. In Shepherdstown, an Italian named Giuseppe Minghini, who had come to America as valet of the famous Major General Charles Lee of Leetown, through he laughed at Livingston's complaints, informed him that the minister must be a Catholic priest and directed him to the estate of a distinguished Catholic family named McSherry. Late that evening Mrs. McSherry saw Mr. Livingston, whose farm was about four miles away, coming toward her house, and she met him at the gate. When he asked to see the priest, she told him there was no priest there then, but that one would "hold church" at a home in Shepherdstown the following Sunday morning.

According to local traditions, this Mr. Richard McSherry, who is to play an important part in our story, with his devout wife and children, had come to America after making a fortune in trade in Jamaica. It is said that "he was of fine personal appearance, dressing carefully in the fashion of his day, with lace ruffles, powdered hair, and silver knee buckles. Genial and kind in manners, he exercised a generous and elegant hospitality."

On the next Sunday, the McSherry's met Mr. Livingston in the Catholic home in Shepherdstown, and as soon as the priest, Father Dennis Cahill of Hagerstown, appeared at the altar vested for Mass, the old Lutheran farmer suddenly burst into tears and exclaimed "That is the very man I saw in my dreams — he is the one who will relieve me!" When the Mass was over, going right to the priest, he poured out his sad story and earnestly begged him for help. At first Father Cahill, who was a very busy and practical man, though that Mr. Livingston was suffering from delusions, and he said with a laugh that his neighbors were just playing jokes on him and that he should go home and watch out for them. But Mr. McSherry and Mr. Minghini, moved by the old farmer's sincerity and suffering, persuaded Father Cahill to visit the haunted house with them.

The priest questioned the whole Livingston family, but they all told him exactly the same story. He therefore consented to say some prayers and to sprinkle the house with Holy Water. As he was leaving, a sum of money that had lately vanished mysteriously from the farmer's locked chest, was suddenly laid by invisible hands on the door-sill between the priest's feet!

Now the Livingston home became quite for several days. But soon the weird noises and dreaded clipping started again. So Father Cahill came a second time and celebrated Holy Mass in the house, after which the various disturbances ceased — for good!

The old Lutheran farmer was so deeply grateful for having obtained the relief which had been promised him, that he thereupon decided to accept the Catholic religion with all his family. Indeed, as Msgr. Matthew Smith wrote in one of his two columns on Father Gallitzin, in the Register (July 20, 1947), "God, it would seem, willed that this anti-Catholic family should be converted to the Catholic Church by seeing what priests could do."

It was at this time, in the fall of the year 1797, that a very remarkable young priest was sent by his superiors to investigate these strange happenings at Cliptown: the twenty-seven year old Father Demetrius A. "Smith," who was born Prince "Mitri" Gallitzin, the son of a German countess and a Russian prince-ambassador of the Empress Catherine the

Great. Only ten years previously he had been converted to the Catholic church, and in 1795 he had been ordained by Bishop Carroll, being the first priest to receive all his orders in this country. Later, during his forty years of holy and heroic service to God at Loretto, Pa., he was to become famous as the great "Apostle of the Alleghenies." While visiting the Livingstons and the McSherrys, he wrote a thorough account of the whole matter, but unfortunately this precious manuscript was soon lost. However, referring to the Mystery of the Wizard Clip in a letter he wrote to a daughter of the McSherrys on April 11, 1839, one year before his death, Father Gallitzin declared:

> My very dear child and friend:
>
> O! What pleasing recollections you recall to my memory! The happy days I spent in the family of Richard McSherry — Yes, my dearest child, in 1797, I think in September, I became acquainted with your dear parents, and very soon a most intimate friendship was formed _ I remained in that part of the country, spending all my time either at their home or at the Livingston's from September until near Christmas . . .My view in coming to Virginia, and remaining there three months, was to investigate those extraordinary facts at Livingston's, of which I had heard so much. . . and which I could not prevail upon myself to believe; but I was soon converted to a full belief of them. No lawyer in a court of justice did ever examine or cross-examine witness more strictly that I did all those I could procure . . .Rev. Mr. Cahill. instructed them, took them into the church, and finally the work of destruction ceased."

And in another account Father Gallitzin added:

> . . . the old man, having (through the means of a respectable Catholic neighbor) obtained the assistance of a real minister of Christ, found the relief for which he had prayed so fervently; and soon after became a most edifying member of the Catholic Church.

Thus ends the first — but by no means the most marvelous — chapter in the Mystery of the Wizard Clip. Henceforth, through the divine power of the True Church of Christ, the evil spirits were banished, and in their place appeared a Spirit of Light and Truth whose inspiring spiritual guidance brought about profound changes for the good in the lives of the Livingstons, the McSherrys and their neighbors.

One day when the Livingston family was sitting around their living room together, all of a sudden they saw among them a barefooted, poorly dressed man with a beard. They thought he was a beggar. As the day was very cold, Mr. Livingston offered him a pair of shoes and some clothes, which he accepted, though he said that they were not needed where he came from, for there was neither heat nor cold in his country. When they asked him where he came from, he replied: "From my Father." Then they asked him where he was going, and he answered: "To my Father. And I have come to teach you the way of my Father."

This mysterious stranger stayed with them for three days and nights, instructing them in the Catholic religion. As his beard was long, they asked him weather he wanted to shave, and he said: "Yes it is not displeasing to Almighty God to be cleanly."

When he left, Mr. Livingston watched carefully to see where he went, as they had not seen him come in. One of the McSherry girls was sent to open the gate for him. They saw him pass through the gate as she swung it open, and go down into a lot in front of the house. Then, while walking across the open field, he suddenly disappeared from their sight! Thereafter the Livingstons referred to his stay as the visit of the angel.

One evening, after he had been a Catholic for several weeks, Mr. Livingston perceived a dazzling light in one corner of his room, and in an instant the whole house became filled with almost blinding light. And then the old man began to hear a mysterious voice, which instructed him in the sacraments of Penance and Holy Eucharist.

This was but the first in a long series of frequent visitations and lessons from this mystic voice, which as a whole form a far more important element in our story than the devilish clippings.

Often the voice would come and exclaim: "I want prayers!" It would awaken Mr. and Mrs. Livingston at night and tell them to pray hard for perseverance and for sinners. Sometime it made them pray for three hours, though they admitted that it did not seem to be more than a few minutes. And it would suddenly summon them whole family in the evenings with these words "Come — take your seats!" and then it would instruct them very thoroughly in the various dogmas of the Catholic religion.

It emphasized that although they could not see the person who was speaking to them, they should always obey the visible voice which was the priest. Some of the young children are reported to have seen the author of the voice. It revealed to Mr. Livingston that it had once been in the flesh as he was, and that if he persevered he would know whom it was before his death. But he must have taken the secret to the grave when he died in 1820. After the voice had sung three times very beautifully in Latin and in English, the Livingstons naturally though that their mysterious visitor had perhaps been a priest. And indeed during the next seventeen years the voice acted as a wise but strict spiritual director for the Livingston and McSherry families.

Whenever it came —sometimes accompanied by the bright light, it would say, as they made the Sign of the Cross: "—Three great Names! None greater on earth! None greater in Heaven!" Once it ordered the Livingstons to keep a forty-day's fast with three hours of prayer each day. It also commanded them to keep the fourth of March each year as a special holy day, in thanksgiving for their conversion. And it was on that day, at the end of the forty days' fast, that Mr. Livingston heard it sing so beautifully, as also on one All Souls Day.

Every night the voice would join the family in their prayers, saying the Rosary with them, and instructing them how to pray well. It also explained the Mass to them, and stated that "one Mass was more acceptable to Almighty God than all the sighs and tears of the whole world put together, for it was God, a pure God, offered up to God."

It stressed what a blessing it is for us to have a merciful Mother of God as our Advocate, and that she has great power on behalf of poor sinners. And because Mrs. Livingston, who had been a Lutheran, was somewhat stubborn about honoring the Blessed Virgin, the voice insisted that in the second part of the Hail Mary they say: "Holy, Holy, Holy Mary, Mother of God . . ."

Once when one of the Livingston girls went to confession and failed to mention a certain sin through shame, the voice not only told the whole family that she had not mentioned it, but reminded her of it and pressed her to confess it as soon as possible.

One day when Mr. Livingston was working in the fields with his sons, all of a sudden he was apparently taken ill, for they saw him turn deathly pale and double up. As they helped him to walk home, he explained that he had just heard a soul in Purgatory screaming for help. And later he often said that he could never forget that shriek — it had been so dreadful.

One night the voice made the Livingstons get up three times to pray for a certain soul in Purgatory. And when one of the girls began to think that after all the souls could have saved themselves and they deserved their pains and anyhow the whole thing was exaggerated, suddenly they all heard a voice shrieking, "Help! Help!" when asked what kind of help was needed, it replied "Prayers, for we are in excruciating torments. Hand me something and you will be convinced!" And as soon as a shirt was held up, a whole human hand was burned into it, leaving the spaces between the fingers not scorched. The entire family saw both the flame and the hand. On another occasion the letters IHS were cleanly burned in deep red colors on a vest. These supernaturally marked objects, as well as some of the clipped cloth, were kept and seen by many persons for over thirty years, although unfortunately they were all eventually lost or destroyed.

When Mrs. McSherry asked where the soul of her former confessor was, expecting to hear that he was long since in Heaven, as he had been a very holy priest who had died seventeen years before, the voice replied: "Father F- is still detained in the scorching flames of Purgatory, on account of some carelessness in the management of some property of orphans he had charge of. He trusted it to someone else, and did not see to it that it was properly attended to.

Early one morning Mr. Livingston went over to the McSherry estate and told Mrs. McSherry that the voice had just informed him that her sister, Mrs. Mary Spalding, had died at about midnight in Baltimore, that she was in Purgatory "for over-indulgence to her children", and that Masses should be offered for her soul. Several days later a letter arrived from Baltimore announcing the death of Mrs. Spalding at the very hour mentioned by the voice. Mrs. McSherry had eighty Masses said for her sister. And one day when she was walking to the Livingston's with her husband, the gates were all opened for them to pass through, without anyone touching them. The voice explained that "Mrs. Mary Spalding had opened them."

The mystic voice from the other world always placed just as much stress upon living a true Christian life as upon praying for the souls in Purgatory. It strongly recommended hospitality, and it often severely warned the Livingstons and the McSherrys against the vanities of the world and especially against fashion. It urged the wealthy McSherrys to set aside all pride and vanity and to humble themselves to the earth, as though they were sackcloth and ashes. It informed them that some of their relatives who had been long detained in Purgatory because of their worldliness, "very much lamented their children being so worldly and so full of worldly grandeur." It claimed that ruffles and fringes, flounces and tuckers and "modesty pieces" (lace worn over the bosom) were all inventions of Satan. Our Lord had come to meek and lowly, it asserted, and so how could we, sinful worms of the earth, deck and adorn our sinful bodies? It declared that thousands of persons were burning in hell forever because of grievous sins that had resulted from their wishing to follow the fashions of the world. Once when three McSherry girls were fitting on some new dresses and admiring themselves, the large mirror before which they were standing was suddenly shattered into hundreds of tiny pieces! In this connection, it is certainly significant that Father Gallitzin, who was intimately acquainted with the teachings of the voice, always strongly opposed any ostentation in his parishioners, especially in the dress of women at church, and he frequently preached against such display.

The voice often spoke of the grave troubles that were hanging over the world, and it told Mr. Livingston to inform Mrs. McSherry that "she would not live to see it, but her children would — war, pestilence, and famine!" It added that those of the family who would remain faithful to God would not suffer from these scourges, and that they would know when they were in God's favor. And as a matter of fact, during the Civil War, none of the eight sons and daughters received the slightest injury, except for one son who died from over-exertion in his work in a military hospital.

As was only to be expected, these extraordinary events and revelations resulted in the conversion of many friends and relatives of the two favored families. In fact, during one winter fourteen persons are known to have joined the Catholic Church in the region around "Priest's Place," as the Livingston property now came to be called. And the Catholics nearby of Maryland and Virginia were inspired to lead better lives, particularly when they saw that the Livingsons and the McSherrys, under the guidance of the mystic voice, had become ardent lay-apostles of Christ.

In January 1800, when the protestant wife of the some what lax Catholic, Mr. Joseph Minghini, fell dangerously ill, at the bidding of the voice, Mrs. McSherry visited and consoled her. After they had repeated an Act of Contrition together, the dying woman seemed to be truly penitent and ready to see a priest. But her husband protested that she had her own preachers and that there was no priest within forty miles. Finally however, as the voice had urged and predicted, Father Gallitzin was summoned and he received Mrs. Minhini into the church. The voice had also specified that the messenger would meet both Father Cahill and Father Gallitzin, but that the later was the one intended for the woman, "as being of a milder nature." A few weeks later, in a letter to Bishop Carroll, Father Gallitzin described the conversion as "miraculous". When Mrs. McSherry returned home, she dreamed that she saw a little child strike a great rock with a stick, whereupon the stone crumbled to dust. The next morning the voice informed her through the Livingstons that Mrs. Minghini had died during the night and that her sins had crumbled away, like the rock, as a result of her sincere contrition and the priest's absolution.

Another striking incident, however, served as a vivid warning against waiting for a deathbed conversion. The protestant wife of a Catholic man in Winchester being near death and having finally asked for a priest, a messenger was sent to the McSherry's estate and found the priest there. But when they searched for the priest's horse, Old Bull, in a small nearby field called Spring Pasture, where it had been seen only a few moments before, no one could find the horse! After considerable searching and delay, on of Mr. McSherry's horses was saddled, and the priest left. Soon afterwards Old Bull was heard neighing and was found in the middle of Spring Pasture, to the utter amazement of the thirty persons who had just searched for him in vain. Then Mr. Livingston was told by the voice that the horse had been there all the time but had been made invisible, because the woman put off her conversion until the last moment, that she had died before the priest could reach her — as was subsequently confirmed — and that Almighty God had permitted this as a warning to the living not to depend on a death-bed repentance.

In August 1804, Mr. McSherry nearly died of a severe illness. Having had some unpleasant difference with Father Cahill, he had not been to confession and communion for some time. But now the voice told Mr. Livingston to go to Mr. McSherry and "his dear helpmate," as it always called his wife (according to Father Gallitzin), and to tell them that Mr. McSherry should "humble himself and go to confession, and touch Christ through the church, and he would be cured." The apparently dying man immediately sent for Father Cahill, and that same night, which his family thought would be his last, he made his confession, received Holy Communion, made his thanksgiving, and then fell into a peaceful sleep.

The next morning he was up before anyone else, and when his family saw him walking around the house, some of them at first thought he was a ghost. Actually, though still pale and emaciated, he was completely cured, and he lived until September 7, 1822.

A lady in a certain family had a brother who was studying for the priesthood in Georgetown College. Through Mr. Livingston, the voice informed this lady that her brother, whom it called "my son", had become a blasphemer who openly proclaimed that he believed in neither the real presence of Christ in the Blessed Sacrament nor the power of the Church to forgive sins. The voice added that if he died in that state of mind, he would open his eyes in the raging flames below, among the damned, and that no prayers or good works could help him then. But it insisted that the family's prayers could help him now and that they should pray as fervently for him as they had for their dead parents. It also commanded his sisters and brothers to go to him and fall upon their knees and say to him: "In the Name of The Father and of the Son and of the Holy Ghost, why will you not believe that there is a God, and that nothing is hard or impossible to Him, and that it is as easy for Him to give us His Precious Body and Blood as to give us a cup of cold water?" But the young man remained obstinate in his sins, and eventually, as the voice foretold, he came to a violent end in great poverty: he was thrown from a horse and died of a broken neck.

Mr. Livingston's second wife, despite the fact that she heard the voice more frequently than anyone except her husband, was never sincerely converted. She herself used to say that she was the Judas of the family, and she constantly tried to falsify whatever the voice said. One Thursday evening when some meat-soup was left after dinner, she decided to serve it on Friday, and she therefore locked it in the cellar. But the next morning she found the pot in which she had left the soup was filled with exactly the same quantity of clear water! And the voice told her that it had done it for "it was more proper to take water than to violate the rules of the Church!" The voice also prophesied that she would die in her own home and room, and so when she became ill she deliberately left the house, in order to prove the voice wrong, and went to live with a Quaker family, whose daughter happened to be dying. This girl told Mrs. Livingston that she wanted some spiritual help but did not know just what it was that she needed. The voice informed Mrs. Livingston that it was Baptism and urged her to arrange for it. After the girl died with out being baptized, the voice told Mrs. Livingston that this would appear against her on Judgment Day. And when she was near death, she was obliged by circumstances to beg to be taken home, where she died in her own room, just as the voice had foretold.

One of the Livingston girls, Eve, became a very saintly woman. However, once after joining the Catholic Church, she went to a protestant meeting, and while there she was moved to tears at the sight of so many persons who did not know anything of the true church. But the voice reproved her for going to the meeting, saying that she "had committed a great sin, as the people thought she was affected by what she heard — they did not know her thoughts." Eve Livingston spent much of her time with the devout old Mrs. McSherry, and after she died "in the odor of sanctity," the voice declared that "her soul did not even pass though Purgatory."

When Mr. Livingston's son Henry came of age, he refused to do the reaping unless his father paid him regular harvest wages. But very soon he was taken with a pain in his knee, which became so swollen and infected that he was confined to bed for eighteen months. After he had suffered that length of time, the voice announced that "he had satisfied the Justice of God for his disobedience and disrespect to his father," and the young man was healed. He must have taken this severe lesson to heart, for it is recorded that he too lived a very holy life henceforth. On the other hand, Father Gallitzin wrong that some of the other Livingston children, "I believe care very little for the church."

Mrs. McSherry, "the dear helpmate," had at least two remarkable mystical experiences. One day she was frightened at seeing a cradle[2] containing her infant son William being rocked violently without anyone touch it. Later the voice told her through Mr. Livingston that "it was the devil who was trying to destroy the child, knowing that he would one day be his enemy." And in fact, that child became Very Reverend William McSherry, one of the Provincials of the Society of Jesus in the United States.

One Sunday Mrs. McSherry stayed home with a sick child while the rest of the family went to church. As she was praying for her child in an upstairs room, she suddenly saw "a beautiful person standing before her in a light cloud, which one had up and the other down, and a nail running through each hand, who said to her: 'Whatsoever you do for one of my little ones, you do it for Me.'" She told no one about this marvelous vision, until the priest informed her that the voice had described it to Mr. Livingston.

One night the good old farmer and his daughter Charlotte were sitting together, when the voice spoke from a bright light in a corner of the room and told the girl that the devil had been trying to tempt her all day and would have succeeded, if she had not been holding in her arms all the time a neighbor's baby, but "the innocence of the babe had protected her."

Of course in those times as today many persons refused to believe what they heard about these supernatural events. Once when Mr.

[2]. The cradle is now at Georgetown University, Washington, D. C.

Livingston wanted to warn some acquaintances about their way of living, the voice said: "No, they are like Dives: if they will not hear the church, they will not hear a voice from the dead."

However, soon after his conversion, the former Lutheran went to Baltimore to see Bishop Carroll. The wise and cautious old "Founding Father" of the Catholic Church in the United States, after a thorough examination, declared that "he thought the man had received his knowledge from above." Nevertheless the voice warned Mr. Livingston that many people would not believe these things, that even some priests would laugh and not believe, and that when he saw this, he should not try to convince them.

Mr. Livingston seems to have become especially devoted to Father Gallitzin, whom he visited at Conewago near Gettysburg only a year or two after joining the Catholic Church. He is known to have walked there and back, and the voice told him "that it had been with him the whole way." It is also said, though without conclusive evidence, that through Mr. Livingston the voice disclosed to Father Gallitzin some of his future sufferings and advised him how to bear them. In any case it is a significant fact that, according to Father Gallitzin, "Mr. Livingston removed from Virginia to Bedford County, Pennsylvania, about twenty miles from here (Loretto), where he died in the spring of 1820. I had Mass at his house repeatedly. He continued, to the last, very attentive to his duties, but did not receive the rites of the Church in his last sickness, which carried him off too quick to afford any chance of sending for a priest."

However, before leaving Virginia, on February 21, 1802, as an act of penance and gratitude to God for his conversion, Adam Livingston signed a Deed of Indenture by which he gave thirty-five acres of his land in perpetual trust to the Catholic Church. According to the text of this Deed, which is printed in full in the Appendix and which is on file in the courthouse at Charles Town, Livingston was "conscious to bestow on the said reverend Dennis Cahill some lasting proof of his esteem for him and the religion and principles of which he inculcates and enforces by his example." Livingston named as trustees his friends Richard McSherry, Joseph Minghini, and Clement Pierce. And in the Deed he specified that if it was not possible for Father Cahill or his successors in the region "to reside on the said land and peruse his calling thereupon," then "during every such interval said land is to be rented and the profits thereof are to be applied toward building and repairing a church or chapel thereupon."

Adam Livingston had still another weighty reason for deeding part of his land to the Catholic Church for all time. For one day the voice, that had so often correctly predicted future events, uttered the following striking and significant prophecy:

"Before the end of time, this will be a great place of prayer and fasting and praise!"[3]

Was the voice foretelling the future development on this tract of land of a popular Catholic pilgrimage shrine or the foundation of a community of contemplative farmer-monks such as the Trappists, who are famed for "prayer and fasting and praise"?

After more than a century of forgetful sleep, "Priest Field" near Middleway, West Virginia, is again coming into its own, thanks partly to the automobile.

In 1922 the late Bishop Denis J. O'Connell of Richmond obtained a "momentous" court decision to the effect that Livingston's trust is still valid and that consequently the property still belongs and shall ever

3. A combination by the writer of the two expressions "Prayer and Fasting" and "Prayer and Praise" which are recorded on page 25, 64, and 112 of Father Finotti's book.

belong to the Catholic Church. On All Souls day, in 1922, together with a considerable gathering of priests and faithful from Maryland, Virginia, and West Virginia, Bishop O'Connell celebrated three Masses under a large tent that had been erected on Priest Field. The following year a modest chapel was constructed, thus fulfilling Adam Livingston's original intention. A lady living in Kentucky who had read about the Mystery of the Wizard Clip in the *Catholic Review* of Baltimore and Washington even wrote to the bishop, offering to pay for the chapel.

Every year thereafter a Mass has been celebrated in the Chapel on Priest Field, first on All Souls Day, but in recent years on the Thursday after the third Sunday in August. In 1926 the sermon was delivered by the Reverend Dom Thomas V. Moore, O.S.B., the well-known writer and professor of psychology who recently became a Carthusian monk in Spain. In 1935 the guest-speaker, the Rev. Louis A. Wheeler, S.J., declared in his sermon:

> God wants simple faith. A Catholic acknowledges that God can work miracles. We do not swallow everything quickly; neither do we despise everything in a skeptical manner. We reverently listen and see what grounds there are for belief. That this is holy ground is well attested to by witnesses of piety and truthfulness and common sense. Let us thank God for this place and pray God that it may be appreciated.

The 150th Anniversary of the historic events known a the Mystery of the Wizard Clip was commemorated on August 21, 1947 by a Requiem High Mass that was sung in the Chapel on Priests Field by Father Thomas C. Healey, pastor of St. Peter's Church, Harper's Ferry, and a choir of fifteen Marist College seminarians. Marist Father Edward Corrigan, in his sermon, pointed out that the occasion was a constant reminder of the supernatural world.

The years 1947 to 1952 mark the 150th Anniversary of the period between the effective exorcism of the evil clipping spirit by a Catholic priest, and the conversion of the Livingston family, and the deeding of Priest Field forever to the Catholic Church. A Chapel has been erected on Priest Field, as Adam Livingston wished.

These anniversary years may well mark a rebirth of popular interest in this lovely and holy spot which was the scene of one of the most impressive manifestation of divine protection and guidance in all the history of the true church of Christ in the United States.

Perhaps the time is not distant when Priest Field will indeed be a "great place of prayer and fasting and praise."

Appendix:
Adam Livingston's Deed of 1802

Levingston

To: Deed

Cahill Etc.

This Indenture made the twenty first day of February in the year one thousand eight hundred and two between Adam Levingston and Mary his wife of Jefferson county Virginia of the first part the reverend Dennis Cahill of the same county of the second part and Richard McSherry Joseph Minghinni and Clement Pierce also of the same county of the third part. WHEREAS, the said reverend Dennis Cahill is a regular clergyman of the church of Rome and by his exemplary conduct and punctual discharge of the duties belonging to that office hath given particular pleasure to the said Adam Levingston who is also of the same persuasion and is conscious to bestow on the said reverend Dennis Cahill some lasting proof of his esteem for him and the religion the principles of which he inculcates and enforces by his example. Now This Indenture witnesses that the said Adam Levingston and Mary his wife in consideration of the premises and of one dollar current money of the United States of America and to him the said Adam in hand paid by the said Reverend Dennis Cahill at or before the sealing and delivery hereof the receipt whereof is hereby acknowledged and also in consideration of the sum of one dollar like currently money to him the said Adam Levingston in hand paid by the said Richard McSherry Joseph Minghinni and Clement Pierce at or before the sealing and delivery hereof the receipt whereof is hereby acknowledged have and each of them hath grated bargained sold aliened released and confirmed and by these presents they the said Adam Levingston and Mary his wife to each of them doth grant bargain sell alien release and confirm unto the said Richard McSherry Joseph Minghinni and Clement Pierce and their heirs a certain tract or parcel of land lying and being in the county of Berkely aforesaid and bounded as followeth Beginning at two white oak saplings on the east side of Opeckon creek corner to a cretin William Hiett, originally, and running thence down the several courses and meanders of said creek North 34 degrees 30 East 26 poles thence North 55 degrees east 40 poles to a white oak and two Spanish oaks on the east bank of Opeckon in the original line of a certain Jacob Broks, thence with his line South 64 degrees east 76 poles to a white oak standing on the said original line of Jacob Brooks and marked corner to the present survey or tract, thence leaving said line or corner and running south 27 degrees West 67 poles to a small Hickory sapling in a hollow thence leaving said corner and running west 42 ½ poles to a large white oak standing on another original line with the aforesaid William Hyatt another marked corner than leaving said corner and running with the original line upon which it stands to wit, William Hiett, North 4 West 48 poles to a large marked white oak corner to said original tract and also to said William Hyatt thence leaving said corner and running thence South 86 degrees West 34 poles to the beginning containing thirty four acres three quarters and twenty perches to be the same more or less being part of tract of land containing 203 acres granted by Thomas lord Fairfax to the aforesaid William Hiett which grant is dated 12th May 1760 and by said William Hiett conveyed to Edward Thomas and by said Edward Thomas conveyed to Christian G. Fox and by said Christian Fox conveyed to the said Adam Levingston, the conveyances not being before the drawer of this Deed a more full description cannot here be given, and all houses ways buildings improvements hereby conveyed belonging or in anyway appertaining and the reversion and reversions remainder and remainders rents its use and profits thereof and also all the estate right Interest claim and demand of the said Adam Levingston and Mary his wife of in and to the same to have and to hold the same land conveyed with the appurtenances unto the said Richard McCherry, Joseph Minghinni and Clement Pierce and their heirs to the only proper use and behoof of the said Richard McSherry, Joseph Minghinni and Clement Pierce and their heirs forever upon this special trust and confidence that they said Richard McSherry, Joseph Minghinni and Clement Pierce do permit the said reverend Dennis Cahill to reside upon the said tract of land and receive the whole emoluments arising there from without any account by him to be rendered and for his own use during the period of the natural life of the said Dennis Cahill without impeachment for waste and after the decease of the said reverend Dennis Cahill then to permit and suffer each clergyman of the same opinion in religion as shall meet with their approbation to hold and enjoy the same land and receive the emoluments arising there from during his natural life without any account to be rendered by him but calling thereupon and in the neighborhood thereof, and in case a Clergyman qualified as above and one will comply with the above conditions cannot be procured during every such interval said land is to be rented and the profits thereof are to be applied towards building and repatriating a church or chapel thereupon. It is the design of the parties to these present that the trust hereby created shall extend to the survivor or survivors of the said trustees and that the heirs of the last surviving trustee that is the trustee who lived longest shall after his decease execute this trust and then the trust shall descent to their heirs and so on so that there shall still be a descent to their heirs and so on so that there shall still be a trustee or trustees, but if by the changes in life it shall turn out that all the inheritable blood who by this deed are made trustees, fail then the court of the said county of Berkely are authorized to appoint three trustees so that they be members of the church of Rome who when appointed shall have the same powers as the trustees first mentioned, and the said Adam Levingston covenants with the said Dennis Cahill and the trustees that he will do any other act so as completely to carry into effect the design hereof should this writing be deemed insufficient and the said Richard McSherry Joseph Minghinni and clement Pierce covenant for themselves and their heirs with the said Adam Levingston and Dennis Cahill that they will execute the trust hereby reposed in them with Fidelity and Justice.

In Witness whereof the parties have hereunto set their hands and seals the day month and year first within written.

Sealed and delivered in presence of,
Cornelius Kelly
George Levingston
Edward Wells
Adam Livingston
Denns. Cahill
Richard McSherry
Joseph Minghinni
Clement Pierce

At a court held for Jeferson county the 8th day of June 1802, this Indenture was acknowledged by the Adam Levingston party thereto and ordered to be recorded

By the court
Teste Geo. Hite

Recorded in Deed Book No. 1, page 152, in the Court House at Charles Town, West Virginia.

Requiem Mass Marks 150th Anniversary of "Wizard Clip"

Gregorian Chant Echoes Throughout Valley

The singing of the Gregorian Chant by 15 youthful seminarians echoed through the surrounding hills of the lower Shenandoah Valley Thursday as a requiem High Mass was celebrated at Priest Field, Middleway, West Virginia, on the 150th anniversary of "the mystery of Wizzard Clip."

Cows grazed disinterestedly in the pasture outside as 85 of the faithful filled the little chapel situated in the center of a field in an isolated woodland area, seven miles west of Charles Town, West Virginia.

Members of the congregation had hiked along a rocky driveway leading from the highway, then through a gate into the field, and finally had trudged through muddy grass to reach the specially constructed church.

Father Thomas C. Healey, pastor of St. Peter's Church Harpers Ferry, celebrated the Mass for the repose of the souls of the faithful departed and especially for that of Adam Livingston, the Lutheran farmer who in 1897 reported a mysterious clipping of various articles in his house. Mr. Livingston became a Catholic, and historians related he was instructed in the Catholic religion by an invisible voice for a period of 17 years.

Last week's Mass was celebrated on one of two pieces of property left the church by Mr. Livingston. The other parcel, a quarter of a mile away, is the site of the Livingston home, only the foundation of which is now standing.

Faith More Important

Pointing out that miracles are not needed to assure the continuity of the Church, Father Edward Corrigan, in giving the sermon, emphasized that the principal requisite for a good Catholic is faith.

"Blessed are they who have not seen and have believed" he quoted our Lord, and went on to assert that strange happenings occur almost daily at shrines throughout the world, but that the Church leaves it to its members to accept or deny them. There is constant evidence, he said, that we live in a supernatural as well as a natural world.

Father Corrigan, a member of the faculty of Marist College, Washington, D.C., declared that we often hear that the best Catholics are converts. He attributed this to the fact that "they must get down on their knees and say an act of faith." Some people, reared in Catholic homes and taught in Catholic schools, marry and leave the Church. This is because, he said, they went to church because their parents told them to and they received Holy Communion because others did. Every Catholic, the priest asserted, should say an earnest act of faith as a means of realizing the true value of belonging to the religion founded by Christ.

"The annual Mass at Priest Field", Father Corrigan said, "is celebrated for the repose of the soul of Adam Livingston. The occasion is a constant reminder of the supernatural world."

MSGR. MCADAMS PRESENT

Students of Marist College, who have been spending the summer at Marist Camp, Harpers Ferry, sang the responses during Mass, and two other seminarians served as altar boys.

Seated within the sanctuary was Right Rev. Msgr. Edward P. McAdams, pastor of St. Joseph's Church, Washington, who attended the first Mass celebrated in 1922 at Priest Field by the late Bishop Denis J. O'Connell, and who was the person to interest Bishop O'Connell in suing for recovery of the property. One of the trustees had been using the land and had contended that it belonged to him in that possession is effective after payment of taxes for a period of 40 years.

Judge Wood of North Carolina ruled, however, in United States District Court, that the property had been left to the church by Livingston and that "a trust does not die." Msgr. McAdams says the jurist described the decision to Bishop O'Connell "as one of the most momentous" in the history of the Federal Court.

The early part of November is regarded as the anniversary of the manifestations, and the annual Mass was celebrated for a time on November 1. However, the weather frequently was cold at that time, and a change was made to the third Thursday in August. For a time the faithful attended the Mass and gathered in the field afterward for a picnic, but this practice was abandoned, except in the case of a small number who continued the custom last week.

Area Called "Wizard Clip"

The area in which the field is located is known as "Wizard Clip"; there is, in fact, an eating place down the road from the site of the Livingston home, the name of which is "Wizard Clip Inn."

The NCWC News Service, which supplies news to all Catholic newspapers, is devoting considerable space this week to the 150th anniversary Mass and the *Jefferson Republican*, a semi-weekly newspaper published in Ranson, West Virginia, has been printing the strange tale in installments.

There are Catholics in the area who are firmly convinced of the truth of the "Wizard Clip" story and there are others who have their doubts. As Father Corrigan pointed out in his sermon the Church leaves it to its members to accept or deny strange happenings. Miracles are not necessary for the sustaining of faith.

(Reprinted from The Catholic Virginian, August 29, 1947)

Bibliography

I. Primary Sources

1) Finotti, Rev. Joseph M., S.J., *The Mystery of the Wizard Clip* (Smithfield, West, Va.) Baltimore, 1889. 143.

This invaluable compilation of primary sources contains:

a. P. 1-13, As "first and most authentic document of the series," a 12 page Manuscript from Georgetown College written about the year 1817 by Rev. Thomas Mulledy, S.J. (1779-1860), at the request of Rev. Anthony Kohlmann. It is based on personal interviews between the two Jesuit priests and Mrs. Anastatia McSherry, the "dear help-mate" of the story, "who related it to them" (p. 18).

b. P. 16-22, A Manuscript account written by Rev. Bro. Joseph Mobberly, S.J. (1799-1827), 1825, based on personal interviews in 1812 with Minghini, who "observed that. . . though he never before had given credit to anything of sort, yet he knew not how to disbelieve the Clip History." "He appeared to be perfectly convinced of the truth of this strange history." (p. 20-21).

c. P. 44-76, Seven letters and a historical account written in 1872 by H.S., a granddaughter of Mrs. A. McSherry, based on all the family reminiscences transmitted by Mrs. McSherry and her daughter (eyewitnesses of the events).

d. P. 87-93, The Gallitzin accounts in his letters and writings.

e. P. 93-96, Two incomplete letters from Mrs. A. McSherry to her brother, Samuel Lilly, undated but obviously written during the period of the manifestations.

2) U.S. Bureau of Census. Heads of Families . . . in the State of Pennsylvania in 1790. Washington. Government Printing Office, 1908 (See p. 287, col. 3).

II. Secondary Sources

A. Catholic

Books:

3) Barry, Joseph. *The Strange Story of Harper's Ferry with Legends of the surrounding Country*. Martinsburg, 1903. 223p. (see P. 207-217)

4) Brownson, Sarah M. *Life of Demetrius A. de Gallitzin*. New York, 1873. 444p. (See p. 100-107).

5. Heyden, Rev. Thomas. *A Memoir of the Life and Character of the Rev. Prince Demetrius A. de Gallitzin*. Baltimore. 1869. 200p (See p. 197-200).

6) Lemcke, Rev. Peter H., O.S.B. *Life and Works of Prince Demetrius Augustine Gallitzin*. New York. 1940. 257 p. (see p. 124-126).

7) Mahon, P.J. *Trails and Triumphs of the Catholic Church in America*. Chicago. 1907. 1046 p. (See p. 646-647).

8) Reily, John T. *Holy Year Collections in the Life and Times of Cardinal Gibbons*. McSherrytown, Pa. 1890-1904. 8v. (See v. 6, p. 604-672).

9) Sargeant, *Daniel Mitri or the Story of Prince Demetrius Augustine Gallitzin* (1770-1840.) New York. 1945. 327 p. (See p 113-116 126, 199, 296).

10) Shea, John Gilmary. *History of the Catholic Church within the United States*. New York. 1888. 2v. (see v. 2, p. 287-290.) (Note Shea encouraged Finotti and collected "all I could finding bearing on the affair." See Finotti, p. 138).

Bibliography

Newspapers:

11) *The Leader*. St. Louis, Mo. December 1, 1855.

12) *The Catholic Review*. Baltimore, October 28, 1922. (See p. 1 and 3.)

13) *The Catholic Review.* Baltimore, October 22, 1926. (See p. 2)

14) *The Register* (National Edition) Denver, July 20, 1947. (See p. 6.)

15) *The Catholic Review*. Baltimore, August 15 1947. (See p. 4)

16) *The Catholic Virginian*. Richmond, August 8, 15, and 29, 1947.

17) National Catholic Welfare Conference News Service Press Release. Washington, D. C., September 1, 1947. (See p. 12-16)

18) *The Catholic Virginian*. Richmond, November 5, 1948. (See p. 12- 13.)

B. Non-Catholic

Books:

19) Aler, F. Vernon. *Aler's History of Martinsburg and Berkely County*, West Virginia. Hagerstown, Md. 1888. 438p. (See p. 12-13)

20) Cartmel, T. K. Shenandoah *Valley Pioneers and Their Descendants*. Winchester, Va. 1909. 587 p. (See p. 241-242.)

21) Hardesty, *H. H. & Co. Historical Hand atlas. . . Special History of the Virginias*. Chicago and Toledo. 1883. 208, 36, 29 p. (See Berkely County Supplement, P. 8)

22) *Jefferson County Historical Society Magazine Charles Town*, West Va. December, 1945, v. XI, p. 38.

23) Norris, J. E. Editor. *History of the Lower Shenandoah Valley Counties*. Chicago. 1890. 812p. (See p. 708)

24) *West Virginia Historical Magazine*. Charleston, West Va. January, 1904. (Vol. 4, p 66-70.)

25) U. S. Works Projects Administration. Writer's Program. West Virginia
(American Guide Series.) New York. 1941. 559p. (See p.311-312)

Newspapers:

26) *The Jefferson Republican* (Newspaper) Ransom, West Va. Aug 24 1947. (p. 4)

27) *The Baltimore Sun*. Baltimore. November 5, 1922. (See p. 11) ("Catholic Services Ends Contest Over Haunted Farm".)

28) *Ibid*. November 2, 1924. (Picture of Chapel. "So famous in this ghost story that the little town is known by the name of Clip as wel as Middleway.")

29) *Ibid*. September 23, 1925.

30) *Ibid*. October 3 and 21, 1926.

(Note: For items No. 28-30 the page numbers were not given on clipping examined in the library of Baltimore Sun.)

A List of Other Small Books Available from Loreto Publications

Boy Heroes - Dom Alban Fruth	$4.95
Breaking With The Past - Abbot Gasquét	$5.95
Counsels to Confessors - St. Leonard of Port Maurice	$6.95
The Conversion of Alphonse Ratisbonne - Baron deBussieres	$7.95
The Wisdom of St. Francis De Sales	$4.95
The Dogma of Faith - St. Benedict Center	$4.95
Explanation of the Veni Sancte Spiritus - Fr. Nicholas Gihr	$6.95
The Gift of Self to God - Fr. Nicholas Grou S.J.	$5.95
50 Meditations on the Passion - Fr. Alban Goodier	$5.95
Meet Brother Martin - Fr. Norbert Georges O.P.	$5.95
The Mystical Body and Its Head - Msgr. Hugh Benson	$6.95
Our Lady of Perpetual Help - Fr. Francis Connell, C.SS.P.	$5.95
Poems of Her Heart - Poetry of Virginia Teehan	$6.95
Poems of Joseph Mary Plunkett	$6.95
Treatise on the Spiritual Life - St. Vincent Ferrer	$5.95
Storm Novena	$4.95
The Wife Desired - Fr. Leo Kinsella	$7.95
The Mystery of the Wizard Clip - Raphael Brown	$5.95
The Woman of Genesis - Bro. T.M. Sennott, MICM	$7.95
The Tragedy of James Connolly - Fr. Denis Fahey	$6.95
The Rulers of Russia & the Russian Farmers - Fr. Fahey	$6.95

Loreto Publications
P. O. Box 603
Fitzwilliam, NH 03447
Phone: 603-239-6671
www.LoretoPubs.org